IF PIGS COULD FLY...

AND OTHER DEEP THOUGHTS

IF PIGS COULD FLY...
AND OTHER DEEP THOUGHTS

A Collection of Funny Poems by
BRUCE LANSKY

Illustrated by
STEPHEN CARPENTER

Meadowbrook Press
Distributed by Simon & Schuster
New York

Library of Congress Cataloging-in-Publication Data

Lansky, Bruce.
    If pigs could fly— and other deep thoughts: a collection of funny poems / by
Bruce Lansky; illustrated by Stephen Carpenter.
        p.   cm.
    Includes index.
    ISBN 0-88166-379-4 (Meadowbrook). — ISBN 0-689-83291-5 (Simon &
Schuster)
    1. Children's poetry, American. 2. Humorous poetry, American.
[1. American poetry. 2. Humorous poetry.] I. Title.

PS3562.A564 I37 2000
811'.54—dc21   00-037976
                                                               CIP

Coordinating Editor: Joseph Gredler
Proofreader: Christine Zuchora-Walske
Production Manager: Paul Woods
Desktop Publishing: Danielle White

Published by Meadowbrook Press, 5451 Smetana Drive, Minnetonka, MN 55343

www.meadowbrookpress.com / www.gigglepoetry.com

BOOK TRADE DISTRIBUTION by Simon & Schuster, a division of Simon and
Schuster, Inc., 1230 Avenue of the Americas, New York, NY 10020

04 03 02 01 00   10 9 8 7 6 5 4 3 2 1

Printed in the United States of America

Dedication

The more schools I visit, the more I realize just how much teachers care about their students; how hard they work (before school, in school, after school); how much money they spend on their students (for books, shoes, eyeglasses, hearing aids) out of their own pockets; and how underappreciated they are.

I dedicate this book to teachers everywhere. I want you to know that I appreciate what you are doing. I hope this book will help each of you reach some child who might not otherwise be interested in reading or writing.

Contents

Introduction x

CRAZY, MIXED-UP ME

On the Day That I Was Born 2
On the Night That I Was Born 3
When I Was a Baby 4
I Like My Nose 5
Dirty Socks 6
Oops! 8
I'm Safe 10
Airsick 11
Fortune: Danger 12

SIBLING MADNESS

My Baby Brother 14
Out of Control 15
My Brother Doesn't Like to Share 16
I Want a Younger Brother 17
Throne Room 18
Forgetful 19
Ain't She Sweet 20

PARENTS AND OTHER GEEZERS

Mom's Diet 22
Pear-Shaped 23
Poor Old Uncle Ted 24
A Lesson Learned 25
Still Growing 26
My Grandma's Teeth 27
My Family 28

ANIMALS I HAVE KNOWN

My Dog Has Got No Manners 30
Poopsie 32
Fussy Cat 33
My New Pet 34
Cows in the Kitchen 36
Pigs in Space 37
Zoo Rules 38
Good-bye, Goldfish 40

SCHOOL DAYS

What I'd Cook for My Teacher 42
Why Is Everyone Staring? 43
School Rules 44
I Should Have Studied 46
A Bad Case of Sneezes 46

LOVE AND OTHER DISEASES

Lovesick 48
I Think You're Cute 49
Kiss Me Not 50
UnValentine 50

MY TWISTED IMAGINATION

The Cherry Pit 52
As I Was Walking 53
Zachary Brown 54
A Young Fellow Named Vance 55
Yankee Doodle in Paris 56
Yankee Doodle's Nose Is Running 56
Blow Your Nose! 57
They Are? 58
There Was an Odd Woman 59
Little Miss Muffet 60

WHAT I'VE LEARNED ABOUT LIFE

Bad Hair Day Rap 62
All You Can Eat Rap 63
Bathroom Warning 64
Winter Warning 64
House Rule 65
Mind Your Manners 66
Birthday Rules 68
Today Is Your Lucky Day 70
Birthday Advice 71
When the Bubble Burst 72
On Mother's Day 73
Dumb and Dumber 74
Don't Make Weird Faces 75
Predictable! 76

TIME FOR BED

When I Sleep 78
How I Dress for Bed 79
Don't Suck Your Thumb 80
Menagerie 81

Index 82

Introduction

When I visit schools, I am often asked silly questions. So I often respond with silly answers. For example:

Q. "How old are you?"
A. "I'm older than dirt, which is why I don't have to wash."

There's one question I'm asked a lot that isn't silly at all—and it's a pleasure to answer:

Q. "Where do you get the ideas for your poems?"
A. "Some of the ideas just pop into my head based on experiences I've had. The rest I make up just for fun."

Here are some stories about how a few of the poems in this book came to be:

"Pigs in Space" (page 37) Have you ever been to a pig farm? I drive past a couple of them on my way from Minneapolis to Duluth. They are the foulest-smelling places on earth—which is why I don't think it would be so great if pigs could fly. (Watch out below!)

"Cows in the Kitchen" (page 36) I call this my Wisconsin poem. Once I visited a dairy farm there, and I had to watch my step in order to skip the dessert. (If you read the poem, you'll know what I mean.)

"All You Can Eat Rap" (page 63) While driving home from a school visit, I had supper at a truck stop that served all-you-can-eat meals. I told the manager I was a famous poet and offered her an autographed poem instead of payment. Bad idea! She took the autographed poem, but still charged me full price. (Maybe if I'd rapped the poem instead, she'd have given me a free meal. On second thought, maybe not.)

"Bad Hair Day Rap" (page 62) While driving to a bookstore in Florida, I got a haircut in a barber shop called Sue's Scalp Shop. (No kidding!) I made the mistake of dozing off while Sue was cutting, and I didn't like what I looked like when I woke up. Sue would probably make a lot more money if she sold hats.

"What I'd Cook for My Teacher" (page 42) Students in a classroom I visited helped me cook up the yucky ideas in this poem. We brainstormed about the most disgusting things we could think of to serve a teacher for lunch. The classroom teacher was nice enough to write down the list for me before she got sick.

"Why Is Everyone Staring?" (page 43) I had trouble coming up with an ending to this poem, so I had to be creative. When I perform it at schools, I often pause before the last word to see if anyone can guess it. (Usually not.) Read this poem to your friends and see if they can guess the last word. (Now that this poem is published, the secret's out. I'll have to write a new poem with a surprise ending to read during my school visits!)

"Kiss Me Not" (page 50) A few weeks before Valentine's Day each year, I like to visit schools in Arizona, Florida, or southern California so I can thaw out (I live in the land of 10,000 skating rinks) and demonstrate how easy and fun it is to make up new "Roses Are Red" poems. "Kiss Me Not" popped into my head while I was in sunny Phoenix. You'll find three other "Roses Are Red" poems in the book: "UnValentine" (page 50), "House Rule" (page 65), and "They Are?" (page 58). Read all three and see if you can make one up, too.

"Poor Old Uncle Ted" (page 24) Bill Cosby once joked that the older he got, the less hair he had on his head and the more hair he had in his ears. I thought that was pretty funny…until it started happening to me. ("Bruce" doesn't rhyme with "head," so I named the uncle "Ted" instead.)

Because I write so many poems in the first person, students often ask me this question:

Q. "When I read your poems, I think you must know me. Have we met before?"

A. "I've never met you before in my life. I have ESP."

And when I speak at conferences for reading teachers and media specialists, teachers I've never met before come up to me, shout, "Bruce Lansky, how are you?" and give me a big hug—like they're my long-lost cousins. Maybe they think I know them, too.

Bruce Lansky

P.S. There aren't many poems in the whole universe that can make you laugh more than once. I've scattered some throughout this book. See if you can find them.

Acknowledgments

I would like to thank the following teachers and their students for helping me select the poems for this book:

Marcy Anderson, Dell Rapids Elementary, Dell Rapids, SD; Kate Arthurs, St. Martin's Episcopal School, Metairie, LA; Patty Bachman, Rockford, IL; Mark Benthall, Austin, TX; Camilla Bowlin, Grassland School, Brentwood, TN; Kathy Budahl, L. B. Williams Elementary, Mitchell, SD; Ann Cox, Aldrich Elementary, Omaha, NE; Bonnie Cox, Kolmar School, Midlothian, IL; Sue Danielson, Withrow Elementary, Hugo, MN; Jane Hesslein, Sunset Hill Elementary, Plymouth, MN; Lori Horstmeyer, Dell Rapids Elementary, Dell Rapids, SD; Barbara Knoss, Hanover School, Hanover, MN; Roni Graham, Central Park Elementary, Plantation, FL; Lori Holm, Hale Elementary, Minneapolis, MN; Kate Hooper, Island Lake Elementary, Shoreview, MN; Ann Johnson, McAuliffe Elementary, Hastings, MN; Julie Kaufman, Del Prado School, Boca Raton, FL; Sharon Klein, Clardy Elementary, Kansas City, MO; Maggie Knutson, Orono Middle School, North Long Lake, MN; Carol Larson, Mississippi Elementary, Coon Rapids, MN; Debbie Lerner, Redbridge School, Kansas City, MO; Sarah Lovelace, Groveland Elementary, Wayzata, MN; Karen Mink, Edgewood School, Woodridge, IL; Michelle Myer, Franklin Elementary, Omaha, NE; Jacky Naslund, Johnsville School, Blaine, MN; Jeanne Nelson, St. Mary's Catholic School, Alexandria, MN; Elaine Nick, Gracemor Elementary, Kansas City, MO; Tessie Oconer, Fulton School, Minneapolis, MN; Margaret Ogren, Hazeldale Elementary, Beaverton, OR; Connie Parrish, Mitchell, SD; Mitzi Pearlman, Acres Green Elementary, Littleton, CO; Polly Pfeiffer, Minnetonka Intermediate School, Excelsior, MN; Barb Rannigan, Alta Vista Elementary, Sarasota, FL; Jackie Robie, Blake Highcroft, Wayzata, MN; Ron Sangalang, Sherwood Forest Elementary, Federal Way, WA; Maria Smith, Bass Race Elementary, Crowley, TX; Melody Tenhoff, Cooper School, Hastings, MN; Tim Tocher, Suffern, NY; Cheryl Triefenbach, Belleville, IL; Vicki Wiita, Cumberland School, Cumberland, WI; DeLinda Youngblood, Centralia, IL.

Crazy, Mixed-Up Me

On the Day That I Was Born

On the day that I was born,
My father was so proud.
No other baby in its crib
could scream and cry so loud.

No other baby kicked its covers
to the nursery floor.
No other baby drank its milk
then yelled, "I want some more!"

And when I messed my diapers,
nurses rang the fire bell.
Then firemen with hoses
would spray the nursery well.

I would have been so boring—
so quiet and well-bred,
if the clumsy doctor hadn't
dropped me on my head.

2

On the Night That I Was Born

On the night that I was born,
it was a hot December morn.
The stars were shining bright as day.
The doctor quit and ran away.
When I popped out, my mother cried,
"It's much too cold, get back inside."

3

When I Was a Baby

When I was a baby, I burped a good deal,
most often just after a rather good meal.

I burped after carrots. I burped after peas.
I burped after crackers. I burped after cheese.

Whenever I burped, it was quite a sensation.
My mother applauded my brilliant creation.

She oohed and she aahed. She clucked and she cooed.
But now when I burp mother shouts, "YOU'RE SO RUDE!!!"

I Like My Nose

I'm glad that my nose
points down to my toes,
and doesn't point up to the sky.
For now I can sneeze
just as much as I please,
without getting goo in my eye.

Dirty Socks

My socks were very dirty,
so I washed them in the lake.
It wasn't long before I knew
I'd made a big mistake.

The water changed from clear to mud.
Then fumes began to rise.
And soon a cloud of air pollution
covered up the skies.

When bullfrogs started croaking
and ducks began to quack,
some campers started chanting,
"We want our clean lake back."

I've got a pile of dirty socks.
I'm in an awful bind.
I guess I'll have to bury them.
I hope the worms don't mind.

Oops!

Three coffee cups my mother loved
lie shattered on the floor.
Three ripe tomatoes splattered
when they hit the kitchen door.

Three jumbo eggs are scrambled.
But they're not on a plate.
Three loaves of bread are crumbled.
I'll use the crumbs for bait.

Three Barbie dolls have lost their heads.
Three pepper mills are smashed.
Three goldfish died while doing flips.
Three model airplanes crashed.

Three lettuce heads unraveled.
Three onions came unpeeled.
My parents didn't know who did it
till my sister squealed.

My parents are befuddled.
They think that I've gone nuts.
But there's a simpler explanation:
I'm a juggling klutz.

I'm Safe

When I am on an airplane ride,
I feel so very safe inside.
But in the john, I worry. So,
I flush and yell, "Watch out below!"

Airsick

My OJ is sloshing around in its cup.
I'm sure it will spill if I don't drink it up.

My Corn Flakes are sliding around on the tray.
When I try to spoon some, the bowl slides away.

My head's feeling dizzy; my stomach feels sick.
So pilot, dear pilot, please land this plane quick.

Fortune: Danger

When I grow up I'd like a job
that's filled with lots of danger.
So, I'm starting at the bottom
as my brother's diaper changer.

Sibling
Madness

My Baby Brother

My baby brother is so small,
he's hardly even there at all.
The only way that we can find him
is by the smell he leaves behind him.

Out of Control

"The president will come to town..."
"The price of beans is coming down..."

"I'll love you till the end of time..."
"But shooting ducks should be a crime..."

"We've never had a better sale..."
"We'll have to break them out of jail..."

"The Pope arrived to lead the prayers..."
"The Dallas Cowboys beat the Bears..."

"The temperature is three below..."
"These vitamins will help you grow..."

What's going on? Well, bless my soul!
Baby's got the remote control.

My Brother Doesn't Like to Share

My brother's such a stingy kid.
He will not share his bike.
I ask if I can borrow it,
He says, "Go take a hike."

He will not share his baseball
and he will not share his bat.
He will not share his catcher's mitt.
He will not share his hat.

He will not share his fishing rod,
his bobbers, or his worms.
The only things my brother shares
are streptococcus germs.

I Want a Younger Brother

I want a younger brother:
someone for me to tease,
someone for me to boss around
and order as I please,
someone for me to wake up
every morning with a shout,
someone who will make my bed,
and take the garbage out,
someone to keep my kitten fed
and clean the litter box,
someone to torture (just for fun
I'll make him smell my socks).

Yes, I want a younger brother,
but I hope that he won't be
another stubborn and rebellious
little rascal just like me.

Throne Room

My mother always nags me.
My father always yells.
My brother always teases.
My sister really smells.

My family's so obnoxious.
They won't leave me alone—
unless the bathroom door is locked,
and I am on my throne.

Forgetful

My sister woke up in the morning.
She had to go potty real bad.
I must have forgotten to put the seat down.
She fell in the toilet—how sad.

She yelled and she screamed and she hollered.
There's no doubt that she was upset.
Whenever my sister is nasty to me,
It seems that I always forget.

Ain't She Sweet

My sister's boyfriends
think she's sweet.
But they have never
smelled her feet.

Parents and Other Geezers

Mom's Diet

Whenever Mom goes on a diet,
she cooks weird food and makes me try it.

When she is hungry, she gets cranky.
If I'm not perfect, she might spank me.

She swims, she bikes, she runs, she dances.
I hope she'll soon fit in her pantses.

Pear-Shaped

My dad has a body that's shaped like a pear.
He looks like he fell from a tree.
I hope that when I have gray hair on my head,
no one will say that of me.

Poor Old Uncle Ted

I feel so bad
for Uncle Ted.
There's not much hair
upon his head.
And, what is worse,
he barely hears.
There's too much hair
inside his ears.

A Lesson Learned

One day, my skydiving Uncle Newt
forgot to pack his parachute.
"That's one mistake," said Auntie Jen,
"that he will never make again."

Still Growing

"My how you've grown,"
said my Auntie Sue.
I looked at her waist and said,
"So have you."

My Grandma's Teeth

My grandma's teeth are like the stars.
She keeps them sparkling bright.
And like the stars up in the sky
her teeth come out at night.

My Family

My family really bugs me.
They're batty as can be.
They should be in the loony bin.
Except, of course, for me.

28

Animals
I Have Known

My Dog Has Got No Manners

My dog has got no manners.
I think he's very rude.
He always whines at dinnertime
while we are eating food.

And when he's feeling thirsty
and wants to take a drink,
he takes it from the toilet
instead of from the sink.

He never wears a pair of pants.
He doesn't wear a shirt.
But worse, he will not shower
to wash away the dirt.

He's not polite to strangers.
He bites them on the rear.
And when I'm on the telephone,
he barks so I can't hear.

When I complained to Mommy,
she said, "I thought you knew:
the reason that his manners stink—
he learns by watching you."

Poopsie

My puppy's name is Poopsie
I gave him that name when:
He made a mess. I cleaned it up.
He made a mess again.

Fussy Cat

I didn't clean her litter box,
so my cat got quite upset.
She wouldn't go inside the box,
and now the carpet's wet.

33

My New Pet

I asked my father for a pet.
He said, "I'll take you shopping."
My father took me to a store
where animals were hopping.

He asked me "Which one would you like?"
So I picked out a puppy,
a parakeet, a rabbit,
plus a gerbil and a guppy.

I also picked a monkey
and a yellow Siamese cat,
a turtle, snake, and lizard,
plus a very big white rat.

My dad said, "If you want a pet,
then you will have to feed it."
Instead, I picked a storybook.
I cannot wait to read it.

Cows in the Kitchen

I'd never seen cows in the kitchen.
That's why it was such a surprise
when I went to grandmother's dairy farm,
the cows there made so many pies.

Pigs in Space

If Pigs could fly around in space,
the world would be a stinky place.
To go outside you'd have to bring
your piggy pooper-scooping thing.

Zoo Rules

Don't insult an elephant
by saying, "You look nosy."
It might reach out with its trunk
to turn you topsy toesy.

Never pet a grizzly bear
and by its cage don't linger.
If you wave your arms about
you're apt to lose a finger.

And if you see some lion cubs,
don't let them out to play.
If their mother catches you,
she just might ruin your day.

When you feed the walruses
be careful not to slip.
If you fall in the walrus pond,
it might be your last dip.

Even though you look like one,
don't make friends with a monkey.
If you pal around with apes,
you'll wind up smelling funky.

Don't fill up on candy floss.
or gobble caramel corn.
When the dentist checks your teeth,
you'll wish you'd not been born.

Don't chatter like a chimpanzee
or hop like a kangaroo.
Your folks might think that you're a beast,
and leave you at the zoo.

Good-bye, Goldfish

The day my favorite goldfish died,
I'm not ashamed to say, I cried.
I prayed for its departed soul,
then flushed it down the toilet bowl.

School Days

What I'd Cook for My Teacher

If I cooked hot lunch for my teacher,
I would start out with rattlesnake stew.
Then I'd serve her a centipede salad
And a tall glass of milk mixed with glue.

Next, a seaweed and jellyfish sandwich,
For dessert, an a-chooberry pie.
When she finally finds out what she's eaten,
I hope the old bat doesn't die.

Why Is Everyone Staring?

If you go to school
and find everyone's staring,
perhaps you forgot something
you should be wearing.

If you have no pants on
you won't be arrested,
unless, of course, you are
completely undresseded.

43

School Rules

Do not oversleep and miss the school bus—
you'll be late.
That's a habit teachers generally
don't appreciate.

Never tell your friends at school
that you still wet your bed.
They are sure to tease you,
and you'll wish that you were dead.

Never call your teacher a name
when she's not near you.
Teachers' ears are excellent,
so they can always hear you.

Do not read a textbook when your hands
aren't clean—it's tricky
to separate the pages when the pages
get real sticky.

When you go out for a team
it's always wise to practice.
When you are a substitute,
the bench can feel like cactus.

Do not copy homework from a friend
who is a dummy.
If you do, I'm sure that you
will get a grade that's crummy.

And if your report card's bad,
don't blame it on your buddy.
Kiss up to your parents quick,
or they might make you study.

I Should Have Studied

I didn't study for the test
and now I'm feeling blue.
I copied off your paper
and I flunked it just like you.

A Bad Case of Sneezes

Last night I had the sneezes.
I was really very ill.
My mother called the doctor
who prescribed a purple pill.

At eight o'clock I went to bed.
My mom turned out the light.
I used up one whole box of Kleenex
sneezing through the night.

I sneezed my brains out in my bed.
I didn't get much rest.
So that's the reason, teacher,
that I flunked the spelling test.

Love and
Other Diseases

Lovesick

I wrote a love note to Sarah.
She bought some chocolates for Matt.
He sent six roses to Lisa.
She baked pink cookies for Pat.

He called Samantha "my darling."
She told me, "I love you dear."
Valentine's Day drives me crazy.
I'm glad it comes just once a year.

I Think You're Cute

I think you're cute.
I really do.
I like your face
and figure, too.

I like your eyes.
I like your nose.
Don't change a thing—
except your clothes.

Kiss Me Not

Roses are red.
Violets are blue.
Please don't kiss me.
I've got the flu.

UnValentine

Roses are Red.
Violets are blue.
Sugar is sweet.
Unlike you.

My Twisted Imagination

The Cherry Pit

When eating some cherries
I swallowed a pit.
I wonder if something
will come of it.

Just think how ridiculous
it would be
if I should give birth
to a cherry tree.

As I Was Walking

As I was walking
out one day,
my head fell off
and rolled away.
I really do not
miss my head.
It doesn't bother me.
I'm dead.

Zachary Brown

This is the story of Zachary Brown.
He never grew upward. He only grew down.

He ate lots of junk food and smoked cigarettes.
His diet was worse than you'd feed to your pets.

He never worked out, and he wasn't athletic.
He shrunk every day. Now, he looks quite pathetic.

This story's alarming, but it's all quite true.
Be careful, or it might just happen to you.

A Young Fellow Named Vance

There was a young fellow named Vance
Who wore a disguise to a dance
He was dressed like a cat
In a Dr. Suess hat
When a dog chewed a hole in his pants.

Yankee Doodle in Paris

Yankee Doodle went to France,
With his golden VISA.
But he could not afford to buy
Da Vinci's *Mona Lisa*.

Yankee Doodle's Nose Is Running

Yankee Doodle went to town
with his baby blankie.
Every time he blew his nose
he used it for a hankie.

Blow Your Nose!

Little Boy Blue
please blow your nose.
It drips like a faucet
and sprays like a hose.
Your brother and sister
are getting upset,
so please blow your nose—
'cause you're getting them wet!

57

They Are?

Roses are blue.
Violets are red.
If you agree
you've got rocks in your head.

There Was an Odd Woman

There was an odd woman
who lived in a shoe.
Which, I think you'll agree,
was a dumb thing to do.
Her husband divorced her.
Her kids ran away.
The shoe smells disgusting.
Why on earth did she stay?

Little Miss Muffet

Little Miss Muffet
sat on a tuffet
eating her curds and whey.
Along came a spider
who sat down beside her.
And since she was still hungry,
she ate the spider, too.

What I've Learned about Life

Bad Hair Day Rap

I went to my barber
and sat in his chair.
I asked him politely
to cut off some hair.

I must have dozed off when
he started to cut.
When I woke up my head was
as bald as my butt.

When you go to the barber
do not take a nap.
Or you'll have to cover
your head with a cap.

All You Can Eat Rap

I went to a place
that serves all you can eat,
and now my new shoes
do not fit on my feet.

My hat is too tiny
to fit on my head.
My legs now hang over
the edge of my bed.

So, if you should visit
the very same place,
take my advice, friend,
and don't stuff your face.

Bathroom Warning

When going to the bathroom,
here's one important issue:
Do not sit on the toilet seat
if there's no toilet tissue.

Winter Warning

When you're playing in the snow
and find out you have to go,
don't sit down upon the toilet
with your snowsuit on—you'll spoil it.

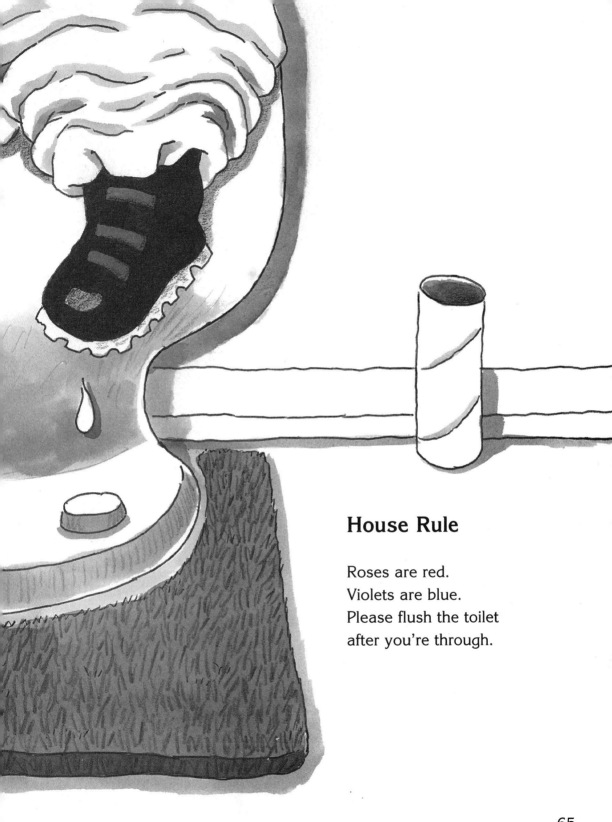

House Rule

Roses are red.
Violets are blue.
Please flush the toilet
after you're through.

Mind Your Manners

Don't drum on the table.
Don't play with your food.
Don't talk while you're chewing;
It's terribly rude.

Don't leave the fridge open.
Don't slam the screen door.
Don't throw dirty laundry
all over the floor.

Don't fight with your brother.
Don't pull the cat's tail.
Don't open your big sister's
personal mail.

Don't pester your parents.
Don't stick out your tongue.
Don't do what your parents did
when they were young.

Birthday Rules

Don't invite your friends who haven't learned to use the potty.
Changing diapers, certainly, will drive your mother dotty.

Don't complain when Grandpa Gus gives you a birthday kiss.
If you're bothered by his beard, just dodge so he will miss.

Don't spill cake and ice cream on your sister's brand-new dress.
Do not start a food fight; you will have to clean the mess.

Don't try to pin the donkey tail on your fat uncle Fred.
Don't ask Auntie Jane's new boyfriend when they plan to wed.

If you get a gift you hate, remember not to swear.
Do not cry when Grandma gives you purple underwear.

If you follow all these rules, your birthday fun will double.
And if you disobey them, you will be in lots of trouble.

Today Is Your Lucky Day

Today on your birthday
consider your luck.
You could have been born
as a pig, cow, or duck.

You could have been born
crying *oink, quack,* or *moo.*
You're lucky you didn't
wind up in the zoo.

Birthday Advice

Today on your birthday
I think you should know—
you're getting too old now
to suck on your toe.

And when you get hungry
I hope you won't spread
the jam that you find
between your toes on your bread.

Do not shine your shoes
with the wax from your ear.
Don't shampoo your hair
with your dad's favorite beer.

Do not chase your nose
when it's running—that's dumb.
When you go to church,
do not dress like a bum.

It's time you grew up
and stopped acting so bad.
It's time that you stopped
acting just like your dad.

When the Bubble Burst

When my bubble gum burst
it was really the worst,
I had gum spread all over my face.
It exploded—went bang—
And my father said, "Dang!"
And my mother said, "You're a disgrace."
Everybody turned round,
when they heard the strange sound—
for the exit I started to search.
So please take my advice,
blowing bubbles ain't nice—
when you're s'posed to be praying in church.

On Mother's Day

On Mother's Day it isn't smart
To give your mom a broken heart.

So here are things you shouldn't say
To dear old mom on Mother's Day:

Don't tell here that you'll never eat
A carrot, celery, bean, or beet.

Don't tell her you think smoking's cool.
Don't tell her you've dropped out of school.

Don't tell her that you've drowned the cat.
Don't tell her that she looks too fat.

Don't tell her when you're grown you'll be
A starving poet—just like me.

Dumb and Dumber

It's dumber than taking a shower,
before you've removed all your clothes.
It's dumber than petting a lion.
It's dumber than picking your nose.

It's dumber than wiping your nose on your sleeve,
then wiping your sleeve on your pants.
It's dumber than dressing in diapers
when you take a date to a dance.

It's dumber than sharing an apple,
with several hungry worms.
It's dumber than sharing a cookie
with a friend who is loaded with germs.

It's dumber than saying that you can't stand
a person whom you've never met.
What's dumber by far than all of these things
is smoking your first cigarette.

Don't Make Weird Faces

Don't make weird faces.
Your face might get stuck.
Then, the rest of your life
you will be out of luck.
You'll look like
a weirdo, a goof, or a geek.
Instead of being normal,
you'll look like a freak—
a freak at the circus
or at the state fair.
People will line up
to point and to stare.
So, don't make weird faces.
It's so very dumb.
You'll look like a freak
and you'll live like a bum.

Predictable!

Poor as a church mouse,
strong as an ox,
cute as a button,
smart as a fox,

thin as a toothpick,
white as a ghost,
fit as a fiddle,
dumb as a post,

bald as an eagle,
neat as a pin,
proud as a peacock,
ugly as sin.

When people are talking,
you know what they'll say
as soon as they start to
use a cliché.

Time for Bed

When I Sleep

It's so hot on the Amazon
I sleep with no pajamas on.
But way up north in Delaware
I sleep in my long underwear.
And when I go to Baltimore,
before I sleep I lock the door.
But when I'm back at home instead,
if I can't sleep I read in bed.

How I Dress for Bed

When winter breezes chill the air,
I sleep in my long underwear.
And if there isn't any heat,
I keep my stockings on my feet.
I climb into my freezing bed
with fuzzy earmuffs on my head.
The reason it's so cold inside:
Mom opens all the windows wide.

Don't Suck Your Thumb

"Don't suck your thumb,"
my mother said.
I answered, "Why?"
and scratched my head.
She said, "It's dumb!
Now go to bed."
That night I sucked
my toe instead.

Menagerie

A pussycat that *quack, quack, quacks.*
A bird that says *meow.*
A doggy that says *oink, oink, oink.*
A duck that says *bow wow.*

A pony that sniffs catnip.
A turkey that eats fries.
A cow that drinks a milk shake.
A turtle that loves pies.

A timberwolf that yodels.
A bear that rides a bike.
An ape that juggles melons.
A pig that loves to hike.

They're just so entertaining—
I like them more than sheep.
I count them and I'm smiling
as I drift off to sleep.

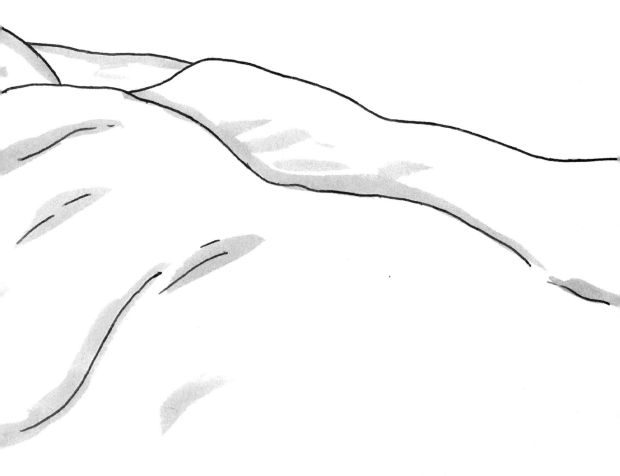

Index

Ain't She Sweet, 20
Airsick, 11
All You Can Eat Rap, 63
As I Was Walking, 53

Bad Case of Sneezes, A, 46
Bad Hair Day Rap, 62
Bathroom Warning, 64
Birthday Advice, 71
Birthday Rules, 68
Blow Your Nose!, 57

Cherry Pit, The, 52
Cows in the Kitchen, 36

Dirty Socks, 6
Don't Make Weird Faces, 75
Don't Suck Your Thumb, 80
Dumb and Dumber, 74

Forgetful, 19
Fortune: Danger, 12
Fussy Cat, 33

Good-bye, Goldfish, 40

House Rule, 65
How I Dress for Bed, 79

I Like My Nose, 5
I'm Safe, 10
I Should Have Studied, 46
I Think You're Cute, 49
I Want a Younger Brother, 17

Kiss Me Not, 50

Lesson Learned, A, 25
Little Miss Muffet, 60
Lovesick, 48

Menagerie, 81
Mind Your Manners, 66
Mom's Diet, 22
My Baby Brother, 14
My Brother Doesn't Like to Share, 16
My Dog Has Got No Manners, 30
My Family, 28
My Grandma's Teeth, 27
My New Pet, 34

On Mother's Day, 73
On the Day That I Was Born, 2
On the Night That I Was Born, 3
Oops!, 8
Out of Control, 15

Pear-Shaped, 23
Pigs in Space, 37
Poopsie, 32
Poor Old Uncle Ted, 24
Predictable!, 76

School Rules, 44
Still Growing, 26

There Was an Odd Woman, 59
They Are?, 58
Throne Room, 18
Today Is Your Lucky Day, 70

UnValentine, 50

What I'd Cook for My Teacher, 42
When I Sleep, 78
When I Was a Baby, 4
When the Bubble Burst, 72
Why Is Everyone Staring?, 43
Winter Warning, 64

Yankee Doodle in Paris, 56
Yankee Doodle's Nose Is Running,
  56
Young Fellow Named Vance, A, 55

Zachary Brown, 54
Zoo Rules, 38

What People Say about Bruce Lansky's Poetry:

What librarians say:

"Bruce Lansky's poetry books are so funny, we can't keep them on our library shelves." —Lynette Townsend, Lomarena Elementary, Laguna Hills, California

"As soon as the library opens in the morning, there is a line of children waiting for Bruce Lansky's poetry books." —Kay Winek, Pattison Elementary, Superior, Wisconsin

What teachers say:

"Some of my students don't like reading, but once they open one of Lansky's poetry books, I can't get them to close it." —Suzanna Thompson, Holy Name Elementary, Wayzata, MN

"Bruce Lansky turns reluctant readers into avid readers."—Sharon Klein, Clardy Elementary, Kansas City, MO

"Bruce Lansky is the 'Pied Piper of Poetry.' He gets children excited about reading and writing poetry."—Mary Wong, Explorer Middle School, Phoenix, AZ

"There's no doubt about it—Bruce Lansky is the king of giggle poetry."—Jody Bolla, North Miami Elementary, Aventura, FL

What critics say:

"Guaranteed to elicit laughs when read alone or aloud to a class."—*Booklist*

"When I read any of his poems, it's giggles galore."—*Instructor* magazine

What kids say about Bruce Lansky's gigglepoetry.com:

"I really like your site. I used to hate poetry, but you guys make it fun."—Christina, Texas

"Even though I'm from outer space, I can speak and read your language. These poems are cool. On my planet, all we ever do is sit around and watch TV." —Me, Outer Space

"I really love this website. It is awesome! It gives me stuff to do when I am grounded." —Tiffany, Enid, Oklahoma

"I think these poems are the best poems ever!!! If you ever get down, they will make you feel better!!! —Hadassah, Augusta, Georgia

"My teacher wanted to read some poems. I gave her some I found on gigglepoetry.com. The whole class laughed like mad zombies." —Jolin, Singapore

Poetry Books by Bruce Lansky:

A Bad Case of the Giggles
Kids Pick the Funniest Poems
Miles of Smiles
Poetry Party

Happy Birthday to Me!
The New Adventures of Mother Goose
No More Homework! No More Tests!
Sweet Dreams

For information about inviting poet/author Bruce Lansky to your school or conference, or to order a free Meadowbrook Press catalog, write or call toll-free:

Meadowbrook Press, 5451 Smetana Drive, Minnetonka, MN 55343, 800-338-2232
www.meadowbrookpress.com   www.gigglepoetry.com